CLAN LINE IN PHOTOGRAPHS

Volume II
From Peace to Peace 1918 - 1945

Compiled by Tony Blacker.

an  publication

Published by:- Avid Publications, Garth Boulevard
Bebington, Wirral,
Merseyside.UK
CH63 5LS
Telephone / Fax: (44) 0151 645 2047
e-mail info@avidpublications.co.uk
website http//www.avidpublications.co.uk

Further copies of this book, and the first volume in the series , *CLAN LINE IN PHOTOGRAPHS - The First 40 Years: 1878-1918* , as well as other Avid Publications are available from the above.

CLAN LINE IN PHOTOGRAPHS - VOLUME II
FROM PEACE TO PEACE - 1918 -1945

by TONY BLACKLER

ISBN 1 902964 0 3 9 © Tony Blackler 2002
A CIP record for this book is available from the British Library

Front Cover: CLAN MACKENDRICK, note railway carriages as deck cargo (see p115)
Rear Cover: CLAN PERTHSHIRE, an early colour photo of a Clan ship. (see p57)

OTHER BOOKS AND VIDEOS AVAILBLE DIRECT FROM AVID PUBLICATIONS
ARE DETAILED AT THE REAR OF THIS BOOK

INTRODUCTION

After the First World War the Cayzer family set about rebuilding the fleet. As Sir Charles Cayzer had died before the Great War had ended this task fell to his sons. August became chairman with Herbert as Vice-Chairman. Harold joined his brothers after the War. The Head Office was moved from Glasgow to 2 & 4, St. Mary Axe, London. The port of registry of Clan Line Steamers Ltd remained at Glasgow to the end.

In 1924 the first Clan Line ship was built by the Greenock Dockyard Co. This yard had come into the Cayzer Empire in 1918. It became a major builder of the company ships until 1966 when it was acquired by Scotts. Greenock Dockyard built the company's first motor ships in 1928 and 1929 but there were no more for some years.

Then came the Great Depression of the late 1920's and early 1930's, followed by the Second World War. During the Depression the company struggled on without laying up any of its ships although many just broke even or even made a loss. The company restructured its capital twice between 1926 and 1932 to meet the conditions. When trade conditions improved, in 1935, the company started a new building programme. Instead of Diesel engines they built two twin-screw, triple expansion engined ships. These were fitted with Bauer-Wach exhaust turbines and six single ended boilers, which could burn either coal or oil. They had a speed of 17 knots. They were designed for the Australian or South African trades and for the trade they were fitted with heavy lift derricks capable of handling complete railway engines. Homeward bound cargoes comprised a large amount of refrigerated consignments of meat, fruit and dairy produce so the holds were capable of carrying this type of cargo. 12 further ships were built before the outbreak of World War II plus another two in 1939. At this time the combined fleet of Clan, Houston and Scottish Shire Line vessels, all now came under the aegis of Cayzer Irvine by 1919. The fleet totalled 400,000 grt and was the largest purely dry cargo fleet in the world.

Sir August Cayzer died in 1943 and was succeeded by Herbert Cayzer. He had been knighted in 1926 for political services as he had become the Member of Parliament for Portsmouth South in 1918 and remained the MP for that constituency until 1939. In 1939 he was elevated to the House of Lords as Lord Rotherwick of Tylney. During the War 36 ships were sunk with the loss of nearly 600 personnel. Many are listed in this volume and many ex Clan Line officers sailed on these ships and several have recently recounted their memories of them to me. For their contribution go my sincere thanks.

Although I have sub-titled this volume 'From Peace to Peace', I have decided that a suitable finishing place for this volume is for the ships built up to about 1943, the end of the 2nd generation of Cayzers. This is the time when the number of ships that were being lost through enemy action was declining and the fleet could start to be rebuilt, just as it did in 1918 where this volume starts. Consequently many of the ships built from then on, which will be in the next volume 'The Final Years', were well known to the many of us that served on them up to the end of Clan Line Steamers Ltd. They were also photographed in colour, unlike most of those built during the era covered by this and the previous volume.

Tony Blackler

ACKNOWLEDGEMENTS

In compiling this, the second of three volumes, of Clan Line ships I wish to acknowledge the invaluable works already in print of the following authors and publications:

Merchant Fleets in Profile (various volumes, principally No. 33) by Duncan Haws.

A Victorian Shipowner (a biography of Charles Cayzer produced for the Clan Line Centenary dinner in 1978) by Augustus Muir and Mair Davies, published by Cayzer, Irvine & Co. Ltd.

In Danger's Hour by Gordon Holman, 1948, published by Hodder & Stoughton Ltd.

Mercantile Navy Lists, many years' editions held in the Guildhall Library, London.

Lloyd's Register of Ships, many years' editions held in Southampton Central Library, Warsash Maritime Centre Library and my own volumes.

British Vessels Lost at Sea 1939-45, HMSO 1947, reprint published by Patrick Stephens 1976.

Clan Line 1878 - 1978 by T. J. Culpin. A thesis lodged in the library of Warsash Maritime Centre, formerly the School of Navigation, Warsash, Hampshire.

Scrap & Build, by D. C. E. Burrell, published by The World Ship Society.

Marine News, 1947 to the present, Journals of the World Ship Society, (WSS).

Sea Breezes, 1919 to the present.

Personal records, Tony Blackler.

Anon. document held in Warsash Maritime Centre Library.

B.E.F. Ships, Before at and After Dunkirk, J. de S. Winser, (WSS 1999)

Kaye, Son & Co. Ltd., K. O'Donoghue & P. M. Heaton, WSS 1983

The Cape Run, W. H. Mitchell & L. A Sawyer, published by Dalton 1984.

NOTES AND ABBREVIATIONS.

If it had not been for the photographs taken and collected by Bob Briscoe and his idea of publishing his collection this work may never have been produced. To his collection I have added my own and I then pondered over how to put them in a logical order. I eventually concluded that they should not be in the same order that many fleet histories use; that of the date upon first entering a company's service. I decided to use the chronological order of the Official Number (O.N.) assigned to the ships upon entering the British Register. As most Clan Line ships were originally registered in Glasgow, this order allows the reader to follow the developments in ship design over a century. The chronological order does not always work, as can be seen with ships acquired from abroad, bought or taken over from other companies and having been registered at other ports.

Many ships were built during World War II and most of these were owned by the Ministry of War Transport (MOWT). They were usually assigned to commercial companies for management purposes and after the war they were sold on or became part of the managing company's fleet. They were often registered at the port preferred by their managers or builder. These ports held blocks of Official Numbers and when they were used up they were given another block. I have indicated the ports of registry for wartime ships whose first port of registry was not Glasgow so the reader can identify those not fully in sequence. That is the reason that some ships listed here appear to be out of order.

Signal letters of many ships changed from 1932 hence some ships are given two sets of signal letters by which all ships are identified, by radio and flags. There are some ships in this which were given wartime signal letters, starting with the letter 'B', which were changed to the usual sequence, starting with the letters 'G' or 'M', later or after the war. I have given both sets where known.

Gross and net tonnages (grt & nrt) are those given for the ship shortly after her first survey. These figures may change considerably and frequently during the life of a ship. They indicate the volumetric size of a ship, 1 ton = 100 cubic feet of space.

Dimensions are generally registered length (between perpendiculars), extreme breadth and moulded depth. These figures are in feet and tenths of feet. They may change over time as ship measurement rules change. After World War II length overall (l.o.a.) is the length usually quoted and where ships lasted until after the war ended I have given the l.o.a. figure. Metric measurements came in later, but I have kept to Imperial measurements for standardisation, as most of the ships were built under that system.

The Summer draught, where given, is the amount of ship under water when she is fully loaded to her Summer loadline and the later ships are shown with the corresponding deadweight tonnage (dwt) in tons.

The engine details are given for engines as built. Over a period of years engines may be modified and re-rated in terms of power. Power terms also changed over the years, as do the methods of calculation. The size of cylinders and the stroke of the pistons usually stayed the same. During this period many ship's engines were changed from coal to oil. This also affected some specifications. After 1957 engine sizes were given in metric measurements and the Nominal Horse Power (NHP) was omitted from the registers. From then, I have given the speed of the ship in knots (nautical miles per hour) as given in the registers.

I have included the builder's yard numbers, where known, as I know many ship enthusiasts like to be given this number as it provides an additional identification and reference for the ship. Like the Official Number (O.N.) it is unique, but unlike the O.N. it cannot be changed. The O.N. often changed with a change of flag.

From 1966 Lloyd's Register of Shipping adopted a new numbering system with six figures known as the Lloyd's Register (LR) number. The first number was a "5". It started in alphabetical order so it will be seen that many Clan ships are in a sequence. Where a LR Number was assigned I have listed it, either with six numbers or seven if the ship was given the added number, which was added after the sixth, in 1968. This unique number is kept for the entire life of the ship and is now known as the IMO (International Maritime Organisation) Number.

Occasionally, an item of data, which should have been included, is not available in the usual sources or does not appear to be correct. Where this occurs a ? is inserted after the heading.

A potted history, if there is anything significant, is given before details of the disposal of all ships. The dates and events are not fully documented here due to space restrictions. Readers may find that some stories catch their attention and these may be followed up in other publications; many of which are mentioned in the Bibliography, but official records, if available, may contain more detail. Sometimes details are given from my own notes made on the ships on which I served, and some have been gleaned from other ex company employees with whom I have had recent contact.

The Author comes from a long line of seafarers, going back at least six generations. In 1959 he went to King Edward VII Nautical College, London and joined British India as a deck cadet in January 1960. He served on many Clan vessels and after gaining his 2nd mates Certificate in 1963; he passed Mates in 1965 and Masters in 1968, all in London. Swallowing the anchor 1983 he joined the staff at Warsash Nautical College as a full time lecturer, teaching mainly seamanship and cargo work.
Tony's other activities include, writing monthly and other articles for *Sea Breezes* Magazine, marine photography, researching family history, and a couple of other maritime related projects.
This is his second compilation of photographs and meticulously researched information in the *'Clan Line in Photographs'* series, having completed Volume I - *'Clan Line in Photographs 1878-1918'* and he has the next and final volume in preparation. He is a member of the Nautical Institute, the World Ship Society, The Thames Ship Society, Shieldhall, and the Paddle Steamer Preservation Society.
His daughter, Ann, is the latest member of the 'Blackler Clan' to take up seafaring. As this book is published she is at sea on a container ship carrying bananas for Great White Fleet.

CLAN LINE IN PHOTOGRAPHS
VOLUME II

Name	**CLAN SKENE**
Ex Name	**WAR ADDER** – launched as
Official Number	141893
Signal Letters	JWDV/GFVM
GRT as built	5257
NRT	3222
Dimensions in feet	401.0 x 52.3 x 28.5
Summer Draught	25' 3¾"
Built by	C. Connell & Co. Ltd.
Year	1919/1
At	Glasgow
Yard Number	389
Engine type	T3 27", 44", 73" - Stroke 48"

NHP   517

Built by   D. Rowan & Co. Ltd.

At   Glasgow

History

1920: transferred to Houston Line. Renamed **HALOCRATES**.

1923: transferred back to Clan Line. Reverted to **CLAN SKENE**.

Disposal

1942, May 10: torpedoed by a submarine in Lat. 31° 43'N Long. 70° 43'W. Nine crew were killed but the Master survived. It was his third survival of a torpedoing.

Photo credit   Briscoe collection & Blackler collection

Name	**CLAN MURRAY (lll)**
Official Number	141894
Signal Letters	JWDT/GQMV
GRT as built	5926
NRT	3678
Dimensions in feet	**loa** 425.0 x 53.5 x 33.5
Summer Draught	26' 4"
Built by	Ayrshire Dockyard Co. Ltd.
Year	1919/1
At	Irvine
Yard Number	472
Engine type	T3 27½", 45½", 75" - Stroke 54"
NHP	413
Built by	Dunsmuir & Jackson Ltd.
At	Glasgow

History

1949: transferred to Houston Line. Renamed **HALIZONES.**

Disposal

1952: scrapped at Bo'ness, Scotland, by P. & W. MacLellan.

Photo credit   Briscoe collection & Blackler collection

Name	**CLAN MATHESON (IV)**
Ex Name	**CLAN MORGAN** – launched as
Official Number	141896
Signal Letters	JWPR/GQMW
GRT as built	5613
NRT	3453
Dimensions in feet	397.1 x 51.4 x 34.0
Summer Draught	27' 5"
Built by	W. Hamilton & Co. Ltd.
Year	1919/4
At	Port Glasgow
Yard Number	311
Engine type	T3 27", 44", 73" - Stroke 48"

NHP   517

Built by   D. Rowan & Co. Ltd.

At   Glasgow

History

1943, December 5: damaged by a direct hit of a bomb from a Japanese aircraft at Calcutta, India. The ship caught fire and was extinguished by the crew. Arrived in the UK in January 1944.

1948: transferred to Houston Line. Renamed **HARMODIUS** (lll)

1951: sold to Tsavliris Shipping Co., London. Renamed **CLAIRE T.**

1955: sold to the Ministry of Transport & Civil Aviation. Renamed **EMPIRE CLAIRE**.

Disposal

1955: loaded with munitions and scuttled in deep water in the Atlantic Ocean.

Photo credit   Briscoe collection .

Name	**CLAN MURDOCH (l)**
Official Number	141911
Signal Letters	KBSL/GQML
GRT as built	5930
NRT	3683
Dimensions in feet	409.5 x 53.5 x 33.5
Summer Draught	26' 7"
Built by	Ayrshire Dockyard Co. Ltd.
Year	1919/7
At	Irvine
Yard Number	473
Engine type	T3 27½", 45½", 75" - Stroke 54"

NHP	560

Built by	Dunsmuir & Jackson Ltd.
At	Glasgow

History

1948: transferred to Houston Line. Renamed **HALESIUS**.
1952: sold to Cia. Capo Bona Esperanza S. A., Panama. Renamed **JANKIKI**.

Disposal

1953, November 28: foundered 50 miles north of Lisbon when her cargo shifted in heavy weather.

Photo credit   Briscoe collection & Blackler collection

Name	**CLAN MACINNES (ll)**
Official Number	141940
Signal Letters	KDLB/GCTP
GRT as built	4672
NRT	2826
Dimensions in feet	384.8 x 52.0 x 26.7
Summer Draught	24' 0"
Built by	Lithgows Ltd.
Year	1920/1
At	Port Glasgow
Yard Number	727
Engine type	T3 27", 44", 73" - Stroke 48"

NHP	517

Built by	Rankin & Blackmore Ltd.
At	Greenock

History

1941, May 4: bombed by aircraft in Liverpool and damaged.

1942: missed by two torpedoes in the Indian Ocean and attacked from the air at Trincomalee, Ceylon.

1942, December: attacked in a convoy in the Mediterranean and shot down a German bomber.

1947: sold to Noemijulia S. S. Co. Ltd., London, (S. Catsell & Co.) Renamed **SAN GEORGE**.

1951: sold to the Indian National S. S. Co. Ltd., Calcutta. Renamed **SIVA-SHAMBHU**.

Disposal

1955: scrapped at Calcutta.

Photo credit   Briscoe collection & Blackler collection.

Name	**CLAN MACWHIRTER (I)**
Ex Names	**YPRESVILLE** - 1919 **HALIZONES** - 1920 **WILLCASINO** - 1923
Official Number	144252
Signal Letters	GDPW
GRT as built	5996
NRT	3757
Dimensions in feet	**loa** 437.0 x 55.2
Summer Draught	26' 3"
Built by	Lloyd Royal Belge (Great Britain) Ltd.
Year	1918/7
At	Whiteinch, Glasgow
Yard Number	3
Engine type	T3 27", 45", 75" - Stroke 48"
Speed	12
Built by	J. G. Kincaid & Co. Ltd.
At	Greenock

History 1918: launched as **YPRESVILLE** for Lloyd Royal Belge.

1919: sold to Cayzer Irvine & Co. Ltd. renamed **HALIZONES**, placed under Houston Line flag.

1920: sold to Convoy S. S. Co., Liverpool. Renamed **WILLCASINO**.

1922: reverted to Houston Line but retained her name.

1923: transferred to Clan Line. Renamed **CLAN MACWHIRTER**.

Disposal

1942, August 26: torpedoed and sunk 100 miles north of Madeira, by **U156**. 10 crew lost.

Photo credit Blackler collection (A. Duncan).

Name	**CLAN FARQUHAR (ll)**
Ex Names	DELPHIC - 1933, MESABA - 1925, WAR ICARUS - 1919
Official Number	142695
Signal Letters	JVPK/GMCX
GRT as built	8002
NRT	4905
Dimensions in feet	450.4 x 58.4 x 37.2
Summer Draught	29' 2¾"
Built by	Harland & Wolff Ltd.
Year	1918/11
At	Belfast
Yard Number	540
Engine type	T3 x 2 26½", 44", 73" - Stroke 48"

NHP   1138

Built by   Harland & Wolff Ltd.

At   Belfast

History

1918: launched as **WAR ICARUS** for the Shipping Controller (Booth Line, manager).

1919: sold to Atlantic Transport Line. Renamed **MESABA**.

1925: sold to White Star Line. Renamed **DELPHIC**.

1933: sold to Cayzer Irvine & Co. Ltd. Renamed **CLAN FARQUHAR (ll)**.

Disposal

1948: towed to Milford Haven, Wales, for scrapping, by T. W. Ward Ltd.

Photo credit   Briscoe collection & Blackler collection.

Name	**CLAN COLQUHOUN (ll)**
Ex Names	**GALLIC** -1933, **WAR ANGUS** - 1919
Official Number	142741
Signal Letters	JVRD/GPYV
GRT as built	7914
NRT	4888
Dimensions in feet	450.0 x 58.5 x 37.1
Summer Draught	29' 2¾"
Built by	Workman Clark & Co. Ltd.

Year 1918 **At** Belfast **Yard Number** 436

Engine type T3 x 2 26½", 44", 73" - Stroke 48" **NHP** 738

Built by Workman Clark & Co. Ltd. **At** Belfast

History

1918: launched for the Shipping Controller as **WAR ANGUS**, (White Star Line as managers).

1919: sold to White Star Line. Renamed **GALLIC**.

1933: sold to Cayzer Irvine & Co. Ltd. Renamed **CLAN COLQUHOUN** (ll).

1947: sold to Zarati S. S. Co., Panama. Renamed **IOANNIS LIVANOS**.

1949: sold to Dos Oceanos Cia. De Nav., Panama. Renamed **JENNY**.

1951: sold to Djakarta Lloyd, Indonesia. Renamed **IMAN BONDJO**.

1952: renamed by the owners to **DJATINEGARA**.

Disposal

1955, December 12: was sent to Osaka, Japan, under tow by **GOLDEN CAPE**, for scrap. Grounded at Lingayen, near Manila, Philippines, on the way.

1956, February 21: refloated and towed to Hong Kong where she was later scrapped.

Photo credit WSPL

Name	**HALIARTUS**
Ex Names	**DENNISTOUN** - 1919 **WAR MOORHEN** – Launched as
Official Number	142832
Signal Letters	KBGW
GRT as built	5294
NRT	3255
Dimensions in feet	400.2 x 52.4 x 28.5
Summer Draught	25' 3"
Built by	J. Readhead & Sons Ltd.
Year	1919/5
At	South Shields
Yard Number	10
Engine type	T3 27", 44", 73" - Stroke 48"

NHP   513

Built by   J. Readhead & Sons Ltd.

At   South Shields

History
1919: launched as the **WAR MOORHEN** for the Shipping Controller and completed for
Shankland, Russell & Co., Glasgow, as the **DENNISTOUN**.
1919: sold to Houston Line. Renamed **HALIARTUS**.

Disposal
1932, May 4: wrecked in fog on Bull Point, 22 miles north of Mossel Bay, South Africa.

Photo credit   Briscoe collection .

Name	**HARMONIDES (ll)**
Ex Name	**HESIONE** - launched as
Official Number	143610
Signal Letters	KDMP/GCKW
GRT as built	5288
NRT	3147
Dimensions in feet	400.2 x 52.3 x 28.5
Summer Draught	25' 3"
Built by	Ayrshire Dockyard Co. Ltd.
Year	1920/1
At	Irvine
Yard Number	484
Engine type	T3 27", 44", 73" - Stroke 48"
NHP	517
Built by	J. G. Kincaid & Co. Ltd
At	Greenock

History
1919: launched as **HESIONE** but completed as **HARMONIDES** in 1920.

Disposal
1942, August 25: torpedoed by a submarine, about 300 miles from Galle, Ceylon, in Lat. 1° 47'N, Long. 77° 27'E. 13 lives lost.

Photo credit   Briscoe collection

Name	**CLAN MACTAGGART (l)**
Official Number	144223
Signal Letters	KHBJ/GDPV
GRT as built	7603
NRT	4776
Dimensions in feet	452.7 x 57.7 x 35.2
Summer Draught	27' 4"
Built by	Ayrshire Dockyard Co. Ltd.
Year	1920/11
At	Irvine
Yard Number	747
Engine type	2 steam turbines coupled to a single screw.
NHP	905
Built by	Scotts Shipbuilding & Engineering Co. Ltd.
At	Greenock

History

1935: transferred to Scottish Shire Line. Retained name.

1940, October 11: damaged by bombs at Liverpool.

Disposal

1942, November 16: torpedoed by a submarine in Lat. 36° 08'N Long. 7° 23'W, about 92 miles from Cape Tarifa, Spain. 175 of the 178 persons on board survived being rescued by a Royal Navy corvette. She was returning home from having taken part in the North African landings.

Photo credit   WPSL

Name	**CLAN MACNAB (lll)**
Official Number	144229
Signal Letters	KHJD/GBYD
GRT as built	6114
NRT	3816
Dimensions in feet	410.6 x 53.3 x 33.4
Summer Draught	27' 9"
Built by	Ayrshire Dockyard Co. Ltd.
Year	1920/12
At	Irvine
Yard Number	485
Engine type	T3 27½", 45½", 75" - Stroke 54"
NHP	560
Built by	Dunsmuir & Jackson Ltd.
At	Glasgow

History

Disposal

1941, March 18: sank off the Cape Verde Islands after having been in a collision with the Norwegian vessel, **STRIX**, during convoy manoeuvres. Fourteen persons were lost.

Photo credit   A. Duncan

Name	**CLAN MACINDOE (l)**
Official Number	144233
Signal Letters	KHLG/GDXN
GRT as built	4635
NRT	2775
Dimensions in feet	384.8 x 52.0 x 26.5
Summer Draught	24' 1"
Built by	Lithgows Ltd.
Year	1920/12
At	Port Glasgow
Yard Number	728
Engine type	T3 27", 44", 73" - Stroke 48"

NHP   517

Built by	Rankin & Blackmore Ltd.
At	Port Glasgow
History	Sister of **CLAN MACINNES** (II).

1941, March: attacked by U boats but escaped.

Disposal

1943, April: caught fire, beached and burnt out at Alexandria, Egypt.

Photo credit   Briscoe collection & Blackler collection

Name	**CLAN MACTAVISH (ll)**
Official Number	144252
Signal Letters	KJFP/GDPW
GRT as built	7619
NRT	4765
Dimensions in feet	452.6 x 57.7 x 29.6
Summer Draught	27' 4"
Built by	Ayrshire Dockyard Co. Ltd.
Year	1921/5
At	Irvine
Yard Number	475
Engine type	2 Steam turbines coupled to a single screw.
NHP	905
Built by	Scotts Shipbuilding & Engineering Co. Ltd.
At	Greenock

History

1942, October 8: rescued survivors of ex-Danish vessel **BORINGIA**, but an hour later she was herself torpedoed.

Disposal

1942, October 8: torpedoed by a submarine in Lat. 34° 53'S Long. 16° 45'E. Only 37 of the 91 crew were saved and of the 35 saved from the Danish ship, **BORINGIA,** 7 persons were lost.

Photo credit   Briscoe collection & Blackler collection

28

Name	**CLAN MACIVER (II)**
Official Number	144253
Signal Letters	KJDT/GFPY
GRT as built	4606
NRT	2751
Dimensions in feet	384.8 x 52.0 x 26.7
Summer Draught	24' 1"
Built by	Lithgows Ltd.
Year	1921/6
At	Port Glasgow
Yard Number	737
Engine type	T3 27", 44", 72" - Stroke 48"

NHP   517

Built by   Rankin & Blackmore Ltd.
At   Greenock

History   Sister of **CLAN MACINNES** (II).
1951: sold to Cia. Maritima Carrena S. A., Costa Rica. Renamed **CARRENA**.
1953: sold to Gulf Steamships, Karachi, Pakistan. Renamed **MUSTALI**.

Disposal
1961: sold for scrap.

Photo credit   Briscoe collection & Blackler collection

Name	**CLAN MACNAIR (l)**
Official Number	144259
Signal Letters	KJGD/GFNK
GRT as built	6094
NRT	3727
Dimensions in feet	410.0 x 53.3 x 33.4
Summer Draught	27' 9¼"
Built by	Ayrshire Dockyard Co. Ltd.
Year	1921/10
At	Glasgow
Yard Number	486
Engine type	T3 27½", 45½", 75" - Stroke 54"
NHP	560
Built by	Dunsmuir & Jackson Ltd.
At	Glasgow

History
Sister of **CLAN MACNAB** (III)

Disposal
1952: broken up at Blyth by Hughes, Bolckow Ltd.

Photo credit   WSPL

Name	**HESPERIA**
Ex Names	**PATRIA** - 1919
Official Number	144661
Signal Letters	KGJF/GDKW
GRT as built	3922
NRT	2392
Dimensions in feet	385.8 x 52.5 x 21.5
Summer Draught	22' 11"
Built by	Flensburger Schiffsbau Ges.
Year	1919
At	Flensburg
Yard Number	351
Engine type	T3 28 ¾", 46 $^{7}/_{16}$", 76" - Stroke 48"

NHP   530

Built by   Flensburger Schiffsbau Ges.   **At**   Flensburg

History

1919: completed as **PATRIA** for Hamburg-America Line, Germany. Ceded to Britain with Royal Mail Line as manager.

1921: sold by the Shipping Controller to Houston Line. Renamed **HESPERIA**.

1938: sold to Euxine Shipping Co. Ltd., London. Renamed **CHRISTINE MARIE**.

1947: sold to Wallem & Co., Hong Kong. Renamed **COSTA RICA**.

1947, September: sold to Paul Kåhre, Helsinki, Finland. Renamed **LEDSUND**.

Disposal

1959, November 21: arrived at Hong Kong for breaking up.

Photo credit   Briscoe collection

Name	**HESPERIDES (lll)**
Ex Name	**PARTHIA** - 1919
Official Number	144694
Signal Letters	KGMT/GDLR
GRT as built	3928
NRT	2378
Dimensions in feet	382.4 x 52.7 x 22.5
Summer Draught	22' 7"
Built by	Flensburger Schiffsbau Ges.
Year	1919
At	Flensburg
Yard Number	353
Engine type	T3 28¾, 46 ²/₅", 76" - Stroke 48"

NHP   527

Built by   Flensburger Schiffsbau Ges.

At   Flensburg

History

Completed for Hamburg-America Line, Germany, as **PARTHIA** but ceded to Britain.

1921: sold to Houston Line by the Shipping Controller. Renamed **HESPERIDES.**

1937: sold to Fisser & Doornum, Emden, Germany. Renamed **BERTHA FISSER**.

Disposal

1939: scuttled off Iceland to avoid capture by the British.

Photo credit   Briscoe collection.

Name	**CLAN MACNAUGHTON (ll)**
Official Number	146259
Signal Letters	KJTB/GFZS
GRT as built	6110
NRT	3784
Dimensions in feet	410.5 x 53.3 x 33.4
Summer Draught	27' 9¼"
Built by	Ayrshire Dockyard Co. Ltd.
Year	1921/10
At	Irvine
Yard Number	488
Engine type	T3 27½", 45½", 75" - Stroke 54"
NHP	561
Built by	Dunsmuir & Jackson Ltd.
At	Glasgow

History   Sister to **CLAN MACNAB** (III).

Disposal

1942, August 1: torpedoed by **U155** in Lat. 11° 54'N Long. 54° 25'W, when bound for Trinidad, West Indies. Five crew were killed.

Photo credit   A.Duncan collection

Name	**CLAN MACNEIL**
Official Number	146281
Signal Letters	KLRC/GFWP
GRT as built	6111
NRT	3788
Dimensions in feet	410.5 x 53.3 x 33.4
Summer Draught	27' 9¼"
Built by	Ayrshire Dockyard Co. Ltd.
Year	1922/2
At	Irvine
Yard Number	489
Engine type	T3 27½", 45½", 75" - Stroke 54"
NHP	560
Built by	Dunsmuir & Jackson Ltd.
At	Glasgow
History	Sister to **CLAN MACNAB** (III).

Disposal

1952: scrapped by Smith & Houston, Glasgow.

Photo credit   Briscoe collection & Blackler collection

Name	**CLAN MACFARLANE (ll)**
Official Number	146317
Signal Letters	KMWH/GJCY
GRT as built	6222
NRT	3850
Dimensions in feet	418.1 x 53.4 x 33.6
Summer Draught	27' 9"
Built by	Ayrshire Dockyard Co. Ltd.
Year	1922/11
At	Glasgow
Yard Number	491
Engine type	T3 27½", 46½", 78" - Stroke 54"
NHP	630
Built by	Dunsmuir & Jackson Ltd.
At	Glasgow
History	Near sister of **CLAN MACNAB** (III). The "Clan F's" were slightly longer.

Disposal

1940, July 17: she sank in five minute after a collision with **GANGES** of Nourse Line, in rough weather, off Socotra Island, Indian Ocean. About half the crew plus 20 out of 24 Askari soldiers were lost.

Photo credit   Briscoe collection & Blackler collection .

Name	**CLAN MACFADYEN (ll)**
Official Number	146335
Signal Letters	KNWL/GDKZ
GRT as built	6224
NRT	3864
Dimensions in feet	418.2 x 53.4 x 33.6
Summer Draught	27' 9"
Built by	Ayrshire Dockyard Co. Ltd.
Year	1923/5
At	Irvine
Yard Number	490
Engine type	T3 27½", 46½", 78" - Stroke 54"
NHP	630
Built by	Dunsmuir & Jackson Ltd.
At	Glasgow
History	

Disposal

1942, November 11: torpedoed by **U508** in Lat. 8° 57'N Long. 59° 48'W, about 100 miles from Trinidad. She sank in 90 seconds and 79 were lost. The survivors spent six days on a raft.

Photo credit   Briscoe collection & Blackler collection

Name	**CLAN MACILWRAITH (l)**
Official Number	147931
Signal Letters	KRSN/GFJP
GRT as built	4958
NRT	2928
Dimensions in feet	387.4 x 52.2 x 27.6
Summer Draught	24' 8¼"
Built by	Greenock Dockyard Co. Ltd.
Year	1924/11
At	Greenock
Yard Number	403
Engine type	T3 27 ⅛", 44", 73" - Stroke 48"
NHP	557
Built by	McKie & Baxter, in 1917
At	Glasgow

History
1950: sold to F. A. Vinnen, Bremen, Germany. Renamed **MAGDALENE VINNEN**.
1956: sold to Cia. Nav. Vapistis S. A., Puerto Limon, Costa Rica. Renamed **SAN GEORGE**.

Disposal
1958: scrapped at Antwerp, Belgium.

Photo credit   Briscoe collection

Name	**CLAN MACDOUGALL (ll)**
Official Number	160234
Signal Letters	LCSJ /GSTB
GRT as built	6843
NRT	4079
Dimensions in feet	454.0 x 62.3 x 28.9
Summer Draught	27' 5½"
Built by	Greenock Dockyard Co. Ltd.
Year	1929
At	Greenock
Yard Number	415
Engine type	B&W 8 cylinder 4 stroke compound double acting; 26¾" bore x 55 $^{1}/_{8}$" stroke.
NHP	1100
Built by	J. G. Kincaid & Co. Ltd.
At	Greenock

History

Clan Line's second motorship.
She was fitted with a 125 tons SWL derrick and unusually for the time she had an "Iron Mike" auto-pilot.

Disposal

1941, May 31: torpedoed by **U106**, near the Cape Verde Islands, in Lat. 16° 50'N Long. 25° 10'W.
2 killed.

Photo credit   Blackler collection

Name	**CLAN MACPHERSON (lll)**
Official Number	160249
Signal Letters	LDHR/GKBW
GRT as built	6940
NRT	4078
Dimensions in feet	454.0 x 62.3 x 28.9
Summer Draught	27' 5½"
Built by	Greenock Dockyard Co. Ltd.
Year	1929
At	Greenock
Yard Number	416
Engine type	T3 30", 50", 83" - Stroke 54" + a low pressure turbine
NHP	973
Built by	Rankin & Blackmore Ltd.
At	Greenock
History	Sister to **CLAN MACDOUGALL** (II), (but she was a steamship).

Disposal

1943, May1: torpedoed by a submarine in the Gulf of Guinea, Lat. 7° 58'N Long. 14° 14'W, 75 miles from Freetown, Sierra Leone. Four engineer officers lost after the crew reboarded in a vain attempt to save the ship.

Photo credit   Blackler collection

Name	**CLAN MACALISTER (lll)**
Official Number	161909
Signal Letters	LFVP/GQYP
GRT as built	6787
NRT	4081
Dimensions in feet	453.8 x 62.3 x 28.9
Summer Draught	27' 5½"
Built by	Greenock Dockyard Co. Ltd., which came into Cayzer Irvine's ownership that year.
Year	1930
At	Greenock
Yard Number	418
Engine type	T3 27", 45", 74" - Stroke 54"
NHP	719
Built by	J. G. Kincaid & Co. Ltd.
At	Greenock
History	

Disposal

1940, May 29: bombed and set on fire by aircraft off Dunkirk, France, whilst being used as an auxiliary transport during the evacuation of the British Expeditionary Force from Dunkirk. Eighteen were killed.

Photo credit   Blackler collection

Name	**CLAN MACARTHUR (lll)**
Official Number	164066
Signal Letters	GYPG
GRT as built	10528
NRT	6105
Dimensions in feet	477.1 x 66.2 x 40.2
Summer Draught	30' 1"
Built by	Greenock Dockyard Co. Ltd.
Year	1936/1
At	Greenock
Yard Number	423
Engine type	T3 x 2 26", 42" 73" - Stroke 48" + 2 low pressure turbines.

NHP	1552

Built by	North East Marine Engine Co. Ltd.
At	Newcastle-upon-Tyne

History

The first twin screw ship built for the company, the first over 10,000 grt and the fastest yet built.

Disposal

1943, August 11: torpedoed by a German submarine in Lat. 23° 00'S Long. 53° 11'E, east of Madagascar. There were 99 survivors from a crew of 151. They took to the few remaining intact boats, had a conversation with the U-boat's crew and were rescued by a French sloop on August 13.

Photo credit   Briscoe collection & Blackler collection

Name	**PERTHSHIRE**
Official Number	164087
Signal Letters	GYWK
GRT as built	10496
NRT	6121
Dimensions in feet	477.1 x 66.2 x 40.2
Summer Draught	30' 0" at 9637 dwt.
Built by	Greenock Dockyard Co. Ltd.
Year	1936/7
At	Greenock
Yard Number	424
Engine type	T3 x 2 26", 42", 73" - Stroke 48" + 2 low pressure turbines
NHP	1585
Built by	North East Marine Engine Co. Ltd.
At	Newcastle
History	Sister of **CLAN MACARTHUR**.

1941, March 23: damaged by bombing at Grand Harbour, Malta.

1963: transferred to Houston Line.

1964: sold to Margalante Cia. Nav. S. A., Piraeus, Greece. Renamed **BORIAS**.

Disposal

1965: sold for scrap in Japan.

Photo credit   Briscoe collection & Blackler collection

Name	**CLAN MACAULAY (ll)**
Official Number	164100
Signal Letters	GZCS
GRT as built	10492
NRT	6118
Dimensions in feet	477.1 x 66.2 x 40.2
Summer Draught	30' 0"
Built by	Greenock Dockyard Co. Ltd.
Year	1936/11
At	Greenock
Yard Number	425
Engine type	T3 x 2 26", 42", 73" - Stroke 48" + 2 low pressure turbines.

NHP   1585

Built by   North East Marine Engine Co. Ltd.
At   Newcastle-upon-Tyne

History   Sister to **PERTHSHIRE** (II) and **CLAN MACARTHUR** (III).
1941, January 19: sustained minor damage from a near miss bomb at Malta. The bomb fell where the ship had been but she had dragged anchor in a gale.
1961: transferred to Houston Line. Retained name.
Disposal
1963, December: arrived at Dalmuir for scrapping by W. H. Arnott Young & Co.

Photo credit   Briscoe collection & Blackler collection

Name	**CLAN CAMERON (III)**
Official Number	164108
Signal Letters	GZGK
GRT as built	7243
NRT	3659
Dimensions in feet	463.7 x 63.0 x 29.9
Summer Draught	28' 4"
Built by	Greenock Dockyard Co. Ltd.
Year	1937/12
At	Greenock
Yard Number	426
Engine type	T3 x 2 26", 42", 68" - Stroke 48" + a low pressure turbine
NHP	1362
Built by	J. G. Kincaid & Co. Ltd.
At	Greenock

History

1945, December 12: the first Clan Line ship to arrive in the UK in peacetime colours.

Disposal

1959: arrived at Hong Kong for breaking up.

Photo credit   Briscoe collection & Blackler collection .

Name	**CLAN CAMPBELL (lV)**
Official Number	164112
Signal Letters	GZLT
GRT as built	7255
NRT	3662
Dimensions in feet	463.7 x 63.0 x 29.9
Summer Draught	28' 4"
Built by	Greenock Dockyard Co. Ltd.
Year	1937
At	Greenock
Yard Number	453
Engine type	T3 x 2 26", 42", 68" - Stroke 48" + a low pressure turbine
NHP	1043
Built by	J.G. Kincaid & Co. Ltd.
At	Glasgow

History   Sister to **CLAN CAMERON** (III).

1942, February 13: bombed by aircraft and damaged in Lat. 32° 22'N Long. 24° 22'E. Sent to Tobruk, Libya, for repairs.

Disposal

1942, March 23: bombed by aircraft 245° x 8 miles from Filfola Island, near Malta. About 30 crew were killed.

Photo credit   Briscoe collection & Blackler collection.

Name	**CLAN KENNEDY (III)**
Ex Name	**OCEAN VISCOUNT** - 1948
Official Number	165840 (registered at Newcastle)
Signal Letters	MAQK
GRT as built	7174
NRT	4272
Dimensions in feet	**loa** 441.5 x 57.0 x 34.8
Summer Draught	26' 11"
Built by	Todd-California S. B. Corp.
Year	1942/6
At	Richmond, California
Yard Number	23
Engine type	T3 24½", 37", 70" - stroke 48"
Speed	12
Built by	General Machinery Corp.
At	Hamilton, Ontario.
History	Sister to **CLAN KEITH** (II).

1942: launched as **OCEAN VISCOUNT** for the Ministry of War Transport (MOWT) with Bibby Bros. as managers.

1948: Acquired by Cayzer Irvine & Co. Ltd. Renamed **CLAN KENNEDY**.

1959: sold to Eddie S. S. Co., Keelung, Taiwan. Renamed **KELLY**.

Disposal

1960: broken up in Japan.

Photo credit WSPL.

Name	**CLAN CHATTAN (ll)**
Official Number	165907
Signal Letters	GZYT
GRT as built	7262
NRT	3666
Dimensions in feet	463.7 x 63.0 x 29.9
Summer Draught	28' 4"
Built by	Greenock Dockyard Co. Ltd.
Year	1937/7
At	Greenock
Yard Number	456
Engine type	T3 x 2 26", 42", 68" - Stroke 48" + a low pressure turbine
NHP	1362
Built by	J. G. Kincaid & Co. Ltd.
At	Greenock

History   Sister to **CLAN CAMERON** (lll).
1942: took part in Operation Tiger in the Mediterranean.

Disposal
1942, February 2: bombed by aircraft in Lat. 35° 01'N Long. 20° 11'E, central Mediterranean.

Photo credit   Briscoe collection.

Name	**CLAN CHISHOLM (ll)**

Official Number	165915
Signal Letters	GBGS
GRT as built	7256
NRT	3617
Dimensions in feet	463.7 x 63.0 x 29.9
Summer Draught	28' 4"
Built by	Greenock Dockyard Co. Ltd.
Year	1937
At	Greenock
Yard Number	457
Engine type	T3 x 2 26", 42", 68" - Stroke 48" + a low pressure turbine

NHP	1043

Built by	J. G. Kincaid & Co. Ltd.
At	Greenock

History   Sister to **CLAN CAMERON** (lll).
First Clan Liner to be sunk in WW2.

Disposal

1939, October 17: torpedoed by a submarine in approximate position, Lat. 45° N 15° W, in the Bay of Biscay. Three of the four boats' occupants were rescued by the Swedish ship, **BARDALAND** and landed at Kirkwall, Orkney Islands. Another 63 were lost.

Photo credit   WSPL

Sixty-three native seamen are missing after the sinking of the Glasgow steamer Clan Chisholm (7,256 tons). **25/10/39**

The owners said to-day: " We understand that only seventeen of the native crew of eighty have been rescued. All the European officers were saved."

The Clan Chisholm was sunk off the Spanish coast, presumably by a U-boat, while on a homeward voyage to Britain. She had a crew on board of 100, made up of 20 Europeans and 80 Lascars.

The vessel was commanded by Captain S. G. Stenson, of Dublin, a merchant service aide-de-camp to the King.

About ten of the European crew belong to Glasgow and other parts of Scotland.

The Clan Chisholm was owned by Clan Line Steamers, Ltd. (managers, Cayzer, Irvine and Co., Ltd.), and was built at Greenock. She was launched in 1937 by Countess Jellicoe, and was registered at Glasgow.

Name	**CLAN CUMMING (ll)**
Official Number	165924
Signal Letters	GDGW
GRT as built	7264
NRT	3676
Dimensions in feet	463.7 x 63.0 x 29.9
Summer Draught	28' 4"
Built by	Greenock Dockyard Co. Ltd.
Year	1938/1
At	Greenock
Yard Number	459
Engine type	T3 x 2 26", 42", 68" - Stroke 48" + a low pressure turbine
NHP	1370
Built by	J.G. Kincaid & Co. Ltd.
At	Greenock
History	Sister to **CLAN CAMERON** (lll).

1940, October 11: bombed by aircraft and damaged at Liverpool, UK.

1941, January 18: torpedoed and damaged by a submarine off Piraeus, Greece. She was more than two months in Piraeus in dry dock. Damaged in Piraeus, by debris, when the **CLAN FRASER** blew up.

Disposal

1941, April 14: mined off Athens, Greece. Rescued by a Greek destroyer, **QUEEN OLGA**. So started a 2 month long hike, for the Master and his crew, across Greece and the Mediterranean before getting home – a long story in itself.

Photo credit   Briscoe collection.

70

Name	**CLAN BUCHANAN (III)**
Official Number	165929
Signal Letters	GJGL
GRT as built	7266
NRT	3692
Dimensions in feet	**loa** 487.6 x 63.0
Summer Draught	28' 4"
Built by	Greenock Dockyard Co. Ltd.
Year	1938/2
At	Greenock
Yard Number	431
Engine type	T3 x 2 26", 42", 63" - stroke 48" + a LP turbine, double reduction geared.
Speed	12½
Built by	J. G Kincaid & Co. Ltd.
At	Greenock
History	

Disposal

1941, April 28: sunk by the German raider **PINGUIN** in Lat. 5°24'N Long. 62° 46'E, west of the Maldives. Only 13 out of the 104 on board survived her sinking and that of the **PINGUIN** where they had been imprisoned.

Photo credit   WSPL.

Name	**CLAN FERGUSON (ll)**
Official Number	165937
Signal Letters	GLLJ
GRT as built	7347
NRT	3563
Dimensions in feet	463.7 x 63.0 x 29.9
Summer Draught	28' 4¼"
Built by	Greenock Dockyard Co. Ltd.
Year	1938
At	Greenock
Yard Number	432
Engine type	T3 26", 42", 70" - Stroke 48" + a low pressure turbine
NHP	878
Built by	J. G. Kincaid & Co. Ltd.
At	Greenock
History	

Disposal

1942, August 12: torpedoed by aircraft 20 miles north of Zembra Island, Mediterranean, whilst taking part in Operation Pedestal. 64 survived the sinking by taking to rafts. Most of the crew were captured in a variety of ways.

Photo credit   Briscoe collection & Blackler collection .

Name	**CLAN MENZIES (III)**
Official Number	165947
Signal Letters	GMGN
GRT as built	7336
NRT	3555
Dimensions in feet	**loa** 487.6 x 63.0
Summer Draught	28' 4"
Built by	Greenock Dockyard Co. Ltd.
Year	1938
At	Greenock
Yard Number	433
Engine type	T3 x 2 26", 42", 68" - stroke 48" + a LP turbines, double reduction geared.
Speed	17
Built by	J. G. Kincaid & Co. Ltd.
At	Greenock
History	Sister to **CLAN BUCHANAN** (III).

Disposal

1940, July 29: torpedoed and sunk by **U99** off NW Ireland. Six died in the explosion but some of the remainder were picked up by an Irish ship and the rest landed in Ireland with their lifeboat. She had loaded at Melbourne, Australia.

Photo credit   Blackler collection (WSPL).

Name	**CLAN FORBES (lll)**
Official Number	165951
Signal Letters	GPGB
GRT as built	7529
NRT	3495
Dimensions in feet	463.7 x 63.0 x 29.9
Summer Draught	28' 4¼"
Built by	Greenock Dockyard Co. Ltd.
Year	1938/12
At	Greenock
Yard Number	434
Engine type	T3 x 2 26", 42", 68" - Stroke 48" + a low pressure turbine
NHP	1370
Built by	Greenock Dockyard Co. Ltd.
At	Greenock

History

1940, August 14: bombed by aircraft and damaged in Tilbury Docks, UK.

1940: disguised with 2 funnels and real guns, to resemble **HMS MAIDSTONE** on Operation Collar in the Mediterranean.

1942: Depot/repair/supply ship for Addu Atoll base in the Indian Ocean.

Disposal

1959: broken up at Hong Kong.

Photo credit   WSPL.

Name	**CLAN FRASER (lll)**
Official Number	165960
Signal Letters	GPPY
GRT as built	7529
NRT	3524
Dimensions in feet	463.7 x 63.0 x 29.9
Summer Draught	28' 4¼"
Built by	Greenock Dockyard Co. Ltd.
Year	1939/2
At	Greenock
Yard Number	435
Engine type	T3 x 2 26", 42", 68" - Stroke 48" + a low pressure turbine

NHP 1370

Built by J.G. Kincaid & Co. Ltd **At** Greenock

History Sister to **CLAN FORBES** (III).
1940: with **CLAN FORBES** in Operation Collar.

Disposal

1941, April 6: bombed by aircraft at Piraeus, Greece. She was discharging high explosives at the time and she caught fire and blew up. Only seven crew were killed, but enormous damage was done to the port and other ships, including the **CLAN CUMMING**, one of only 2 ships to survive the blast.

This incident was not forgotten in the port and was recounted to the Master and officers of the first and only Clan Line ship to go to Piraeus after the war, the **CLAN MACGILLIVRAY** (ll), in May 1978. *(I was the Chief Officer on her at that time- T.B).*

Photo credit Briscoe collection & Blackler collection

Name	**CLAN LAMONT (III)**
Official Number	165965
Signal Letters	GTTD
GRT as built	7250
NRT	5703
Dimensions in feet	463.7 x 63.0 x 29.9
Summer Draught	29' 0½"
Built by	Greenock Dockyard Co. Ltd.
Year	1939/5
At	Greenock
Yard Number	438
Engine type	T3 x 2 26", 42", 68" - Stroke 48" + a low pressure turbine
NHP	1370
Built by	J. G. Kincaid & Co. Ltd.
At	Greenock

History

1940 – 1948: requisitioned by the Admiralty.

1944, June 5: D-Day -1. She sailed with 1400 Canadian troops for the Normandy Landings, France. In all she made five crossings taking in excess of 8,000 troops.

Disposal

1961: broken up in Japan.

Photo credit   WSPL .

Name	**CLAN MACDONALD (IV)**
LR Number	5075036
Official Number	165971
Signal Letters	GCPG
GRT as built	9653
NRT	5719
Dimensions in feet	**loa** 505.3 x 64.7 x 27.4
Summer Draught	26' 10¾"
Built by	Greenock Dockyard Co. Ltd.
Year	1939/12
At	Greenock
Yard Number	436
Engine type	2 x 10 cylinder 4 SCSA oil
Speed	14
Built by	J. G. Kincaid & Co. Ltd.
At	Greenock

History
1960: transferred to Houston Line but retained name.

Disposal
1970, Aug 6: arrived at Shanghai, China to be broken up.

Photo credit Blackler collection (WSPL).

Name	**LANARKSHIRE**
Official Number	165973
Signal Letters	GCTC
GRT as built	9816
NRT	5822
Dimensions in feet	**loa** 505.3 x 64.7 x 29.9
Summer Draught	28' 6¼"
Built by	Greenock Dockyard Co. Ltd
Year	1940/4
At	Greenock
Yard Number	437
Engine type	Parsons steam turbines x 6, single reduction geared to twin shafts.
Speed	?
Built by	Parsons Marine Turbine Co. Ltd.
At	Newcastle
History	Sister to **CLAN MACDONALD** (IV).

1946: transferred to Scottish Shire Line after the War. Australian service.

1959: transferred to Bullard King & Co. Ltd. Renamed **UMGAZI**.

1960: transferred to Springbok Line. Renamed **GRYSBOK**.

1962: transferred to Safmarine. Renamed **SOUTH AFRICAN FARMER**.

Disposal

1963: arrived Aioi, Japan for breaking up.

Photo credit   Blackler collection (A. Duncan).

Name	**CLAN ANGUS**
Ex Name	**EMPIRE PRINCE** - 1945
Official Number	166214 (registered at Dundee).
Signal Letters	GIFG
GRT as built	7030
NRT	4927
Dimensions in feet	loa 446.3 x 56.3
Summer Draught	26' 9¼" at 10430 dwt.
Built by	Caledon Shipbuilding & Engine Co. Ltd.
Year	1942/5
At	Dundee
Yard Number	394
Engine type	T3 24¼", 39", 70" - stroke 48"

Speed   12

Built by   North-East Marine Engine Co. (1938) Ltd.   **At**   Newcastle

History

Built for the Ministry of War Transport, (Gibbs & Co., Newport, Wales as managers).

1945: acquired by Cayzer Irvine & Co. Ltd., and renamed **CLAN ANGUS**.

1951: converted to oil fuel.

1956: transferred to Bullard King & Co. Ltd., upon the merger into the British & Commonwealth Shipping Group. Renamed **UMKAZI**.

1959: reverted to **CLAN ANGUS**.

Disposal

1962, 22 April: arrived for scrapping at Hirao, Japan.

Photo credit   Blackler collection (WSPL).

Name	**CLAN KEITH (II)**
Ex Name	**OCEAN VERITY** - 1948
Official Number	167858 (registered at Southampton).
Signal Letters	BDXC / GOFV
GRT as built	7174
NRT	4272
Dimensions in feet	**loa** 441.5 x 57.0
Summer Draught	26' 11" at 10490 dwt.
Built by	Permanente Metals Corp. Shipyard No.1
Year	1942/6
At	Richmond, California
Yard Number	24
Engine type	T3 24½, 37", 70" - stroke 48"
Speed	12
Built by	General Machinery Corp.
At	Hamilton, Ontario.
History	Sister to **CLAN KENNEDY** (II).

1946, June: entered service for the Ministry of War Transport (MOWT). Glen Line Ltd, managers.

1948: acquired by Cayzer Irvine & Co. Ltd., Renamed **CLAN KEITH**.

Disposal

1961, 5 November: Struck Ecueils des Soreilles Rocks near Cap Bon, North Africa. Later sank off the Tunisian coast, with the loss of 62 crew, six survived. She was on passage from the UK to India. Clan Line's largest post WW2 loss in terms of lives.

Photo credit   Blackler collection (A. Duncan).

Name	**STIRLINGSHIRE (II)**
Ex Name	**EMPIRE FALKLAND** - 1946
LR Number	534109
Official Number	168536 (registered at Belfast).
Signal Letters	GCQD/GPVA
GRT as built	7006
NRT	4030
Dimensions in feet	**loa** 448.0 x 56.3
Summer Draught	26' 4" on 8834 dwt.
Built by	Harland & Wolff Ltd.
Year	1945/2
At	Belfast
Yard Number	1276
Engine type	B & W 4 stroke single acting, 6 cylinder.
Speed	12
Built by	Harland & Wolff Ltd.
At	Belfast
History	Completed as the **EMPIRE FALKLAND** for the MOWT, (Turnbull Martin as manager).

1946: transferred to Houston Line and renamed **STIRLINGSHIRE**, operated by the Scottish Shire Line, with Clan Line colours.

1966: sold to Van Heyghen Frères' Yard, Belgium, for about £60,000.

Disposal

1966, 5 September: arrived at Bruges for breaking up.

Photo credit   Blackler collection (A. Duncan).

Name	**CLAN MACQUEEN**
Ex Name	**OCEAN VESPER** - 1951
Official Number	168630 (registered at Cardiff)
Signal Letters	BCXZ/MAQG
GRT as built	7174
NRT	4272
Dimensions in feet	**loa** 441.5 x 57.0
Summer Draught	26' 11" at 10490 dwt.
Built by	Todd-California S. B. Corp.
Year	1942/1
At	Richmond, California
Yard Number	6
Engine type	T3 24½", 37", 70" - stroke 48"

Speed   12

Built by   General Machinery Corp.   **At**   Hamilton, Ontario.

History   Sister to **CLAN KEITH** (II).

Completed as the **OCEAN VESPER**. Managed for the Ministry of War Transport (MOWT) by Kaye , Sons & Co.

1951: Sold to Cayzer Irvine & Co. Ltd. Renamed **CLAN MACQUEEN**.

1954: transferred to Houston Line. Renamed **HERMINIUS**.

1958: sold to Pan-Norse S. S. Co. S. A., Panama. Renamed **EKBERG**.

1963: sold to Marine Development & Supply S. A., Panama.

Disposal

1964, 11 December: arrived at Onomichi, Japan, for breaking up by Koshin Sangyo K. K.

Photo credit   Blackler collection (WSPL).

Name	**CLAN MACBRAYNE (II)**
Ex Name	**OCEAN MESSENGER** - 1948
Official Number	168638 (registered at Cardiff).
Signal Letters	BDVN/MAQA
GRT as built	7178
NRT	4280
Dimensions in feet	**loa** 441.5 x 57.0
Summer Draught	26' 10¾"
Built by	Todd-Bath Iron S. B. Corp.
Year	1942/10
At	Portland, Maine, USA
Yard Number	25
Engine type	T3 24½", 37", 70" - stroke 48"
Speed	12
Built by	John Inglis & Co. Ltd.
At	Toronto, Ontario, Canada.
History	Sister to **CLAN KEITH** (II).

1942: owned by the Ministry of War Transport (Watts, Watts & Co., managers)
1948: acquired by Cayzer Irvine & Co. Ltd. Renamed **CLAN MACBRAYNE.**
1960: transferred to King Line.

Disposal
1961, March 27: arrived at Mihara, Japan for breaking up.

Photo credit	Blackler collection (A. Duncan).

Name	**CLAN ALLAN**
Ex Name	**EMPIRE FOREST** - 1945
LR Number	502283
Official Number	168653 (registered at South Shields).
Signal Letters	BDPP/GUFP
GRT as built	7043
NRT	4967
Dimensions in feet	**loa** 446.4 x 56.2
Summer Draught	26' 9"
Built by	J.Readhead & Sons Ltd.
Year	1942/3
At	South Shields
Yard Number	526
Engine type	T3 24½", 39", 70" - stroke 48"
Speed	12
Built by	J. Readhead & Sons Ltd
At	South Shields
History	Sister to **CLAN ANGUS**.

1942, Jan 15: launched for the Ministry of War Transport (MOWT) (Burn Line, manager).

1944: Cayzer Irvine & Co. Ltd., became managers.

1946: renamed **CLAN ALLAN**.

1958: transferred to Bullard, King & Co. Renamed **UMTALI**.

1959: reverted to Clan Line and **CLAN ALLAN**.

1961: sold to Mullion & Co. Ltd., Hong Kong. Renamed **ARDSIROD**.

Disposal

1966, October 12: arrived at Kaohsiung, Taiwan, for breaking up.

Photo credit   Blackler collection (WSPL).

Name	**CLAN MACQUARRIE (II)**
Ex name	**OCEAN WAYFARER** - 1951
Official Number	168636 (registered at Cardiff).
Signal Letters	BDVF/MAQQ
GRT as built	7178
NRT	4280
Dimensions in feet	**loa** 441.5 x 57.0
Summer Draught	26' 10¾"
Built by	Todd-Bath Iron S. B. Corp.
Year	1942/9
At	Portland, Maine, USA.
Yard Number	19
Engine type	T3 24½", 37", 70" - stroke 48"
Speed	12
Built by	Canadian Allis-Chalmers Ltd.
At	Montreal, Canada.
History	Sister to **CLAN KEITH** (II).

1942, September: completed for the MOWT (Thompson S. S. Co. Ltd, Cardiff, managers).

1951: acquired by Cayzer Irvine & Co. Ltd., and renamed **CLAN MACQUARRIE**.

Disposal

1953, January 31: grounded at Port of Ness, 10 miles west of the Butt of Lewis, whilst on passage from Dundee to Glasgow.

1953, March 16: refloated but declared a total loss.

1953, November: broken up at Troon by the West of Scotland Shipbreaking Co. Ltd.

Photo credit   Blackler collection (A. Duncan).

Name	**CLAN KENNETH (II)**
Ex Name	**OCEAN VICEROY** - 1948
LR Number	526341
Official Number	168734 (registered at Glasgow)
Signal Letters	BDXD/MAQH
GRT as built	7174
NRT	4272
Dimensions in feet	**loa** 441.5 x 57.0
Summer Draught	26' 11" at 10490 dwt.
Built by	Todd-California S. B. Corp.
Year	1942/6
At	Richmond, California, USA.
Yard Number	25
Engine type	T3 24½", 37", 70" - stroke 48"
Speed	12
Built by	General Machinery Corp.
At	Hamilton, Ontario, Canada.

History   Sister to **CLAN KEITH** (II).

1942: built for the MOWT (P. Henderson & Co. Ltd., managers).

1943, March 29: damaged by a torpedo from a submarine in Lat. 46° 44'N Long. 16° 38' W.

1948: acquired by Cayzer Irvine & Co. Ltd. Renamed **CLAN KENNETH**.

1958: sold to Cia. Concordia de Nav. S. A., Piraeus, Greece. Renamed **OMONIA II**.

Disposal

1966, April 13: caught fire and beached near Amsterdam. Declared a total loss.

1966, July 15: arrived at Hamburg, under tow, and later scrapped by Eisen & Metall A. G.

Photo credit   Blackler collection (WSPL).

Name	**CLAN CAMPBELL (V)**
Official Number	168761
Signal Letters	GDZK
GRT as built	9545
NRT	5090
Dimensions in feet	loa 486.6 x 63.0
Summer Draught	29' 4½"
Built by	Greenock Dockyard Co. Ltd.
Year	1943/5
At	Greenock
Yard Number	453
Engine type	T3 x 2 26", 42", 68" - stroke 68" + a low pressure turbine.
Speed	15
Built by	J. G. Kincaid & Co. Ltd.
At	Greenock

History

1961 transferred to King Line Ltd.

Disposal

1961, 27 September: arrived at Hong Kong for scrapping.

Photo credit   Blackler collection (WSPL).

Name	**CLAN MACBEAN (II)**
Ex Name	**OCEAN COURIER** - 1948
Official Number	168840 (registered at Liverpool)
Signal Letters	BDVM/MAPV
GRT as built	7178
NRT	4280
Dimensions in feet	**loa** 441.5 x 57.0
Summer Draught	26' 10¾"
Built by	Todd-Bath Iron S. B. Corp.
Year	1942/10
At	Portland, Maine, USA
Yard Number	24
Engine type	T3 24½", 37", 70" - stroke 48"
Speed	12
Built by	Dominion Engineering Works Ltd.
At	Montreal, Canada.

History Sister to **CLAN KEITH** (II).
1942: built for the MOWT (Larrinaga S. S. Co. Ltd, managers).
1944: served at the D-Day beaches.
1948: acquired by Cayzer Irvine & Co. Ltd. Renamed **CLAN MACBEAN**.

Disposal
1960, September 20: arrived at Hong Kong for breaking up.

Photo credit Blackler collection (WSPL).

Name	**CLAN MACKENZIE (IV)**
Ex Name	**EMPIRE CATO** - 1948
Official Number	168949 (registered at West Hartlepool)
Signal Letters	BFLC/GUFU
GRT as built	7039
NRT	4851
Dimensions in feet	**loa** 446.3 x 56.2
Summer Draught	26' 9"
Built by	W. Gray & Co. Ltd.
Year	1942/12
At	West Hartlepool
Yard Number	1138
Engine type	T3 24½", 39", 70" - stroke 48"
Speed	12
Built by	Central Marine Engineering Works (W. Gray & Co. Ltd.)
At	West Hartlepool

History   Sister to **CLAN ANGUS**.
1942: built for the MOWT (Hain S. S. Co. Ltd., managers).
1947: acquired by Cayzer Irvine & Co. Ltd. Renamed **CLAN MACKENZIE**.
1960: sold to Wheelock, Marden & Co., Hong Kong for scrap.

Disposal
1960, October 14: arrived at Hong Kong and broken up.

Photo credit   Blackler collection (A. Duncan).

Name	**CLAN MACRAE (III)**
Ex-Name	**EMPIRE MIGHT** - 1946
Official Number	168986 (registered at Greenock).
Signal Letters	BDXS/MAHP
GRT as built	9209
NRT	4922
Dimensions in feet	**loa** 487.6 x 63.0
Summer Draught	29' 10"
Built by	Greenock Dockyard Co. Ltd.
Year	1942/8 **At** Greenock
Yard Number	450
Engine type	T3 x 2 6", 42", 68" , - stroke 48" + low pressure turbines + double reduction geared to twin shafts.
Speed	16
Built by	J. G. Kincaid & Co. Ltd. **At** Greenock
History	1942: built for the MOWT (Blue Star Line, manager).

1946: acquired by Cayzer Irvine & Co. Ltd., and refitted and renamed **CLAN MACRAE**.

1959: transferred to Bullard, King & Co. Ltd., London. Renamed **UMGENI**.

1960: transferred to Safmarine/Cayzer Irvine's Springbok Line, Cape Town.
        Renamed **GEMSBOK**.

1961, July: transferred to South African Marine Corporation, (Safmarine).
        Renamed **SOUTH AFRICAN FINANCIER**.

1962: sold to Redwijs Baarn N.V., Holland, for a delivery voyage to the breakers.
        Renamed **SANTA MARIA DE ORTAZ**. Resold.

Disposal

1962, February 10: arrived at Valencia, Spain and broken up.

Photo credit   Blackler collection (WSPL).

Name	**EMPIRE BARRIE / CLAN ALPINE (IV)**
Official Number	169016 (registered at Sunderland).
Signal Letters	BDRD/GIFF
GRT as built	7168
NRT	4253
Dimensions in feet	**loa** 441.5 x 57.2
Summer Draught	26' 11¾"
Built by	J. L Thompson & Sons Ltd.
Year	1942/4
At	Sunderland
Yard Number	615
Engine type	T3 24½", 39", 70" - stroke 48"
Speed	11
Built by	George Clark (1938) Ltd. **At** Sunderland

History 1942: launched for the MOWT (Albyn Line, manager), as **EMPIRE BARRIE**.

1944: management transferred to Cayzer Irvine & Co. Ltd, (Clan Line), same name.

1945: acquired by Cayzer Irvine & Co. Ltd. Renamed **CLAN ALPINE**.

1957: transferred to Bullard, King & Co. Ltd, London. Renamed **UMVOTI**.

1959: reverted to Clan Line and **CLAN ALPINE**.

1960, September 16: sailed from the Mersey bound for Onomichi and Japanese shipbreakers, but during the voyage via Chittagong, East Pakistan, she was caught in a cyclone. Whilst at anchor in the Kharnapuli River she dragged anchor and when the floods subsided she was found to have dragged 8 miles up river and was half a mile inland, in a paddy field! Her cargo was discharged in the field.

Disposal

1961: a road was built to the ship and she was cut up on site.

Photo credit Blackler collection (A. Duncan & WSPL).

Name	**CLAN MACKENDRICK**
Ex Name	**EMPIRE PICKWICK** - 1948
LR Number	502280
Official Number	169053 (registered at South Shields).
Signal Letters	GBPS
GRT as built	7068
NRT	4778
Dimensions in feet	**loa** 446.2 x 56.2
Summer Draught	26' 9"
Built by	J. Readhead & Sons Ltd.
Year	1943/11
At	South Shields
Yard Number	536
Engine type	T3 24½", 39", 70", - stroke 48"
Speed	12
Built by	J. Readhead & Sons Ltd.
At	South Shields

History   Sister of **CLAN ANGUS**.

1943: built for the MOWT (Donaldson Bros., Glasgow, managers).

1946: chartered to Clan Line.

1948: acquired by Cayzer Irvine & Co. Ltd. Renamed **CLAN MACKENDRICK**.

1961: sold to Mullion & Co. Ltd., Hong Kong. Renamed **ARDPATRICK**.

1966: sold to the National Shipping Corp., Pakistan. Renamed **HARINGHATA**.

Disposal

1968, July 16: arrived at Gadani Beach, Pakistan, and broken up.

Photo credit   Blackler collection (A. Duncan).

Name	**CLAN MACBRIDE (II)**
Ex Name	**OCEAN GYPSY** - 1948
LR Number	501116
Official Number	169067 (registered at Manchester).
Signal Letters	BDVS/MAPY
GRT as built	7178
NRT	4280
Dimensions in feet	**loa** 441.5 x 57.0
Summer Draught	26' 10¾" at 10490 dwt.
Built by	Todd-Bath Iron S. B. Corp.
Year	1942/11
At	Portland, Maine, USA.
Yard Number	29
Engine type	T3 24½", 37", 70" - stroke 48"
Speed	12
Built by	John Inglis & Co. Ltd.
At	Toronto, Ontario, Canada.
History	Sister to **CLAN KEITH** (II).

1942: built for the MOWT (J. & C. Harrison, London, managers).

1948: acquired by Cayzer Irvine & Co. Ltd. Renamed **CLAN MACBRIDE**.

1958: sold to Wheelock, Marden & Co. Ltd., Hong Kong. Renamed **ALICE**, registered in Panama, (Valles S. S. Co. Ltd.).

Disposal

1966, May 10: grounded near Kuantan, Malaysia.

1966, June 4: refloated.

1966, July 7: arrived at Hirao, Japan, for scrapping.

Photo credit Blackler collection (WSPL).

Name	**CLAN MACBETH (II)**
Ex Name	**OCEAN GLORY** - 1948
Official Number	169176 (registered at Newcastle).
Signal Letters	BDVT/MAPX
GRT as built	7178
NRT	4280
Dimensions in feet	**loa** 441.5 x 57.0
Summer Draught	26' 10¾" at 10490 dwt.
Built by	Todd-Bath Iron Shipbuilding Corp.
Year	1942/11
At	Portland, Maine, USA.
Yard Number	30
Engine type	T3 24½", 37", 70" - stroke 48"
Speed	12
Built by	John Inglis Co. Ltd.
At	Toronto, Canada.

History   Sister to **CLAN KEITH** (II).

1942, November: Completed for MOWT and managed by J. & C. Harrison Ltd., Newcastle.

1948: sold to Cayzer Irvine & Co. Ltd. Renamed **CLAN MACBETH** (II).

1950, August: converted to burn oil fuel.

1959: sold to Wheelock, Marden & Co., Hong Kong. Renamed **MADONNA** by the Oriental S. S. Corp., Panama.

1961: owned by the Sincere Navigation Co., Keelung, Taiwan. Renamed **SINCERE TRADER**.

Disposal

1964, December: broken up at Kaohsiung, Taiwan.

Photo credit   Blackler collection (WSPL).

Name	**CLAN URQUHART (III)**
LR Number	507529
Official Number	169404
Signal Letters	GFBK
GRT as built	9726
NRT	5607
Dimensions in feet	**loa** 500.5 x 65.8
Summer Draught	29' 3¼"
Built by	Greenock Dockyard Co. Ltd.
Year	1944/1
At	Greenock
Yard Number	454
Engine type	T3 x 2 26", 42", 68" - stroke 48" + a low pressure turbine + double reduction gearing to twin shafts.
Speed	16
Built by	J. G. Kincaid & Co. Ltd.
At	Greenock
History	Sister to **CLAN MACDONALD** (IV).

1943, June: launched for Clan Line.

1960: transferred to Houston Line. Retained name.

Disposal

1966, April 8: arrived at Kaohsiung, Taiwan, for scrapping by Chin Ho Fa Steel & Iron Co.

Photo credit   Blackler collection (WSPL).

120

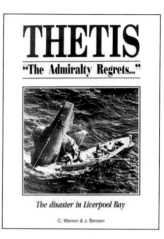

122

THE ALABAMA AFFAIR - The British Shipyards Conspiracy in the American Civil War by David Hollett

This book reveals the turmoil and intrigue surrounding a deal involving the British government, the now defunct Merseyside shipyard of Cammell Laird and a country engaged in civil war, America.

— What was involved? — How was the conspiracy organised?
— Who were the shadowy figures at the centre of the controversy?

The Alabama Affair answers all the questions.

ISBN 1 902964 32 2   £11.50 inc. p&p

BLUE FUNNEL - VOYAGE EAST
by Award Winning author RICHARD WOODMAN

'This is life at sea, warts and all, and a better book because of it.' Sea Breezes

A new and revised version of this classic tale of a typical Blue Funnel Cargo Liner in the middle of the 20th century.
Contains new photographs of many of the 'Blue Flue' vessels.
'The work of a practised writer...a deeply felt...account of merchant shipping in the 1960s...shrewd and readable...' Sunday Times

ISBN 1 902964 0 4 7   £12.50 inc. p&p

LUSITANIA

by Colin Simpson

More than eighty years on the story of the Lusitania continues to be shrouded in mystery and suspicion. What was her real cargo? Why wasn't she protected? Why did she sink so quickly? The Facts, the fictions, but most of all...the truth.

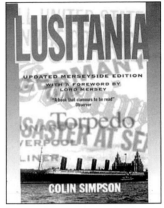

A book that clamours to be read...' - The Observer

ISBN 0 9521020 6 4

£11.00 inc. p&p

FORGOTTEN EMPRESS - The Tragedy of the Empress of Ireland

By David Zeni

'...dubbed 'The 'Forgotten Empress'...the second in a shocking trio of tragedies at sea...sandwiched in between the disasters of the Titanic and the Lusitania, ...it was a sudden death... that sent Liverpool into mourning...' Liverpool Echo

ISBN 1 902964 15 2

£12.50 inc. p&p

THE GOLDEN WRECK - The Loss of the Royal Charter
By Alexander McKee
The effects great of the great hurricane of October 1859 were to
shock the nation. 133 ships were sunk, 90 were badly damaged and
almost 800 people lost their lives.
More than half of those that perished were on one ship - The Royal
Charter.
The worst shipwreck in Welsh history, this is the story of the Royal
Charter...and her gold.
ISBN 1 902964 0 2 0 £11.00 inc. p&p

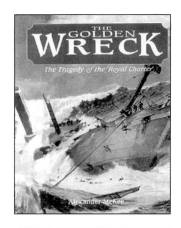

IRON CLIPPER TAYLEUR' ˇ the White Star Lines First Titanic
by H.F. Starkey

'Iron Clipper' is subtitled 'The First Titanic' for it tells the story of
the first White Star liner to be lost on her maiden voyage. The
'Tayleur' tragedy of 1854 and the 'Titanic' catastrophe of 1912 are
disasters which have so much in common that the many coincidences
make this book appear to be a work which is stranger than fiction.
ISBN 1 902964 00 4
£8.00 inc. p&p

LIFE AT LAIRDS - Memories of working shipyard men
by David Roberts
When Cammell Lairds has gone and we are a generation or two down
the line who will answer the questions 'What did they do there?'
'What was it like?' This book answers the questions.
- Sea Breezes

A Piece of Social History ˘ Liverpool Echo
ISBN 0 9521020 1 3
£ 8.00 inc. p&p
{Cammell Laird - Old ships and Hardships: on Video. £14.99 inc. p&p in UK}

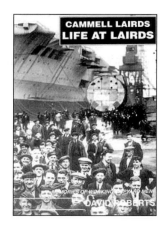

CAMMELL LAIRD - the golden years
by David Roberts.
Foreword by Frank Field MP
'Captures life in the prosperous years of the historic
Birkenhead shipyard'- Liverpool Echo
'Puts into perspective...the strikes...the Polaris
contract...and those who worked at the yard'
- Sea Breezes

ISBN 0 9521020 2 1
£7.50   inc. p&p

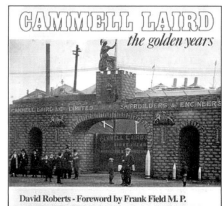

UNION - CASTLE - The Forgotten Navy by Peter Abbott
Features the Intermediate liners, The Royal East Africa Service, Round Africa vessels, coasters, general cargo ships and reefers. Also covers the Zulu War, Boer War, World War I and World War II.
ISBN 1 902964 21 7 £11.00 inc. p&p

LUSITANIA AND BEYOND - the Life of Captain William Thomas Turner
by Mitch Peeke and Kevin Walsh Johnson
Over the years Captain Turner has been accused of treachery, stubbornness, ignorance and much worse. This book gives the true, remarkable story of Captain William Thomas Turner, the last Master of the doomed Lusitania.
ISBN   1 902964 14 4 £9.50 inc. p&p

A WELCOME IN THE HILLSIDES ? - The Merseyside and North Wales Experience of Evacuation by Jill Wallis
A book that is both informative and moving, with the real-life stories of the thousands of children who left the dangers of Merseyside for the safety of North Wales during World War II.
ISBN   1 902964 13 6   £12.00 inc. p&p

THE LIVERPOOL LIFEBOAT DISASTER OF 1892 - One man's search for a missing piece of history -
by Jim Sullivan
'A labour of love that deserves to be told... a story of astonishing courage, brilliantly researched.'
- Alan Bleasdale   ISBN   1 902964 10 1 £8.50 inc. p& p

JUST NUISANCE AB - His Full Story by Terence Sisson
The amazing but true story of the only dog that was officially enlisted into the British Royal Navy, a Great Dane whose name was Nuisance, his official rank and name was AB Just Nuisance. Famed for his preference for the company of navy ratings (he wasn't too keen on Officers) in and around the famous World War II naval base of Simonstown, South Africa, Nuisance helped many a sailor rejoin his ship after a night on the town.   £8.00 inc. p&p

FROM BATTLEFIELD TO BLIGHTY

A History of Frodsham Auxiliary Hospital 1915-1919

by Arthur R Smith

The horrors of the first 'Great War' are well known, but the stories of those sent back from the 'Battlefield to Blighty' tend to be overlooked. This is the little known story in words and photographs of one of the largest auxiliary military hospitals in the country that was established at Frodsham in Cheshire during the First World War.

ISBN 1 9029640 16 0   £8.60 inc. p&p

FASTER THAN THE WIND - A History Guide to the Liverpool to Holyhead Telegraph.

by Frank Large

Take a journey along the one of most spectacular coastlines in Britain, the hills and countryside of North Wales and Wirral. The views are quite superb, and on a clear day it is possible to see just how signals about shipping were sent along the coast to and from Liverpool. This book contains full details of the intriguing and little known sites of the substantial remains of the Liverpool to Holyhead Telegraph Stations.

ISBN 0 9521020 9 9   £10.00 inc. p&p

TO ORDER BOOKS OR VIDEOS DIRECT CONTACT:-

Avid Publications, Garth Boulevard, Hr. Bebington, Wirral, Merseyside UK. CH63 5LS.

Tel / Fax 0151 645 2047

Look at the books and videos via the internet on

http://www.avidpublications.co.uk or   E-mail info@AvidPublications.co.uk

Note. All prices here include postage and packaging within UK.